Here Is Antarctica

Madeleine Dunphy

ILLUSTRATED BY

Tom Leonard

Web of Life
CHILDREN'S BOOKS

**H**ere is Antarctica.

Here are the icebergs
all jagged and spiked
that rise from the sea
in this cold world of ice:
Here is Antarctica.

Here are the seals
who lie on the icebergs
all jagged and spiked
that rise from the sea
in this cold world of ice:
Here is Antarctica.

Here are the orcas
who hunt the seals
who lie on the icebergs
all jagged and spiked
that rise from the sea
in this cold world of ice:
Here is Antarctica.

H*ere are the penguins*

who flee from the orcas

who hunt the seals

who lie on the icebergs

all jagged and spiked

that rise from the sea

in this cold world of ice:

Here is Antarctica.

Here are the krill

that are food for the penguins

who flee from the orcas

who hunt the seals

who lie on the icebergs

all jagged and spiked

that rise from the sea

in this cold world of ice:

Here is Antarctica.

H*ere is the ocean*

that is home to the krill

that are food for the penguins

who flee from the orcas

who hunt the seals

who lie on the icebergs

all jagged and spiked

that rise from the sea

in this cold world of ice:

Here is Antarctica.

Here is the petrel

who floats on the ocean

that is home to the krill

that are food for the penguins

who flee from the orcas

who hunt the seals

who lie on the icebergs

all jagged and spiked

that rise from the sea

in this cold world of ice:

Here is Antarctica.

Here are the penguins

who swim 'round the petrel

who floats on the ocean

that is home to the krill

that are food for the penguins

who flee from the orcas

who hunt the seals

who lie on the icebergs

all jagged and spiked

that rise from the sea

in this cold world of ice:

Here is Antarctica.

Here is the seal

who preys on the penguins

who swim 'round the petrel

who floats on the ocean

that is home to the krill

that are food for the penguins

who flee from the orcas

who hunt the seals

who lie on the icebergs

all jagged and spiked

that rise from the sea

in this cold world of ice:

Here is Antarctica.

Here are the silverfish

that are eaten by the seal

who preys on the penguins

who swim 'round the petrel

who floats on the ocean

that is home to the krill

that are food for the penguins

who flee from the orcas

who hunt the seals

who lie on the icebergs

all jagged and spiked

that rise from the sea

in this cold world of ice:

Here is Antarctica.

Here is the skua

who dives for the silverfish

that are eaten by the seal

who preys on the penguins

who swim 'round the petrel

who floats on the ocean

that is home to the krill

that are food for the penguins

who flee from the orcas

who hunt the seals

who lie on the icebergs

all jagged and spiked

that rise from the sea

in this cold world of ice:

Here is Antarctica.

Here are the penguins
who watch the skua
who dives for the silverfish
that are eaten by the seal
who preys on the penguins
who swim 'round the petrel
who floats on the ocean
that is home to the krill
that are food for the penguins
who flee from the orcas
who hunt the seals
who lie on the icebergs
all jagged and spiked
that rise from the sea
in this cold world of ice:
Here is Antarctica.

H ere are the icebergs

that are home to the penguins

who watch the skua

who dives for the silverfish

that are eaten by the seal

who preys on the penguins

who swim 'round the petrel

who floats on the ocean

that is home to the krill

that are food for the penguins

who flee from the orcas

who hunt the seals

who lie on the icebergs

all jagged and spiked

that rise from the sea

in this cold world of ice:

Here is Antarctica.

Wildlife of Antarctica

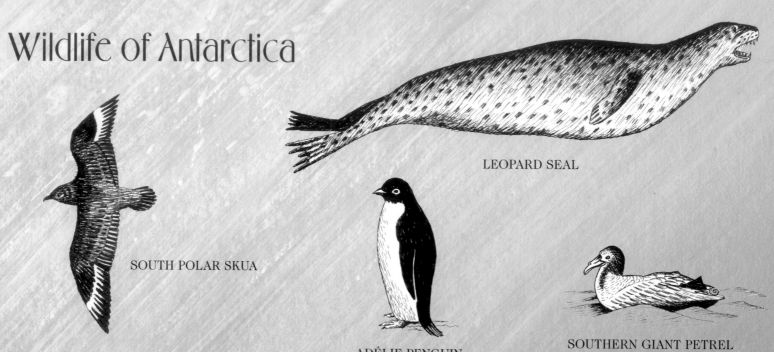

LEOPARD SEAL

SOUTH POLAR SKUA

ADÉLIE PENGUIN

SOUTHERN GIANT PETREL

MACARONI PENGUIN

The continent of Antarctica, approximately twice the size of Australia, lies mainly within the Antarctic Circle and is surrounded by ocean. It is the windiest, driest and coldest place on Earth, with mean winter temperatures ranging from −40 to −70 degrees Celsius (−40 to −94 degrees Fahrenheit). Like the Arctic, Antarctica's winters are dark day and night and its summers are filled with continuous sunlight. This book takes place during Antarctica's summer months.

Antarctica's gigantic icebergs and ice shelves are found nowhere else in the world. Icebergs are not made of frozen salt water; they are born on land and made from fresh water. Icebergs start when snow falls onto land ice. The snow is compressed into more ice over many years and eventually flows toward the sea. Roughly 75% of the world's fresh water is found in Antarctica's ice.

ANTARCTIC SILVERFISH

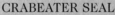

ANTARCTIC KRILL

ORCA

CRABEATER SEAL

Although this spectacular wilderness of snow, ice and rock teems with wildlife, there are no terrestrial mammals native to Antarctica. Most of Antarctica's wildlife can be found on its coasts and in the Southern Ocean. Millions of marine animals, including whales, seals, fish, penguins, and many other bird species make this unique environment their home.

Antarctica faces numerous threats such as climate change, over-fishing and unsustainable tourism. We must act now to help ensure the protection of Antarctica. To find out what you can do, write to the Antarctic & Southern Ocean Coalition, 1630 Connecticut Avenue, N.W., 3rd Floor, Washington, D.C. 20009 or visit their website at www.asoc.org.

EMPEROR PENGUIN

For Jennifer, Caroline, Kathy, Jessie, Suzanne, Beth, Cindy & Amy.
—M.D.

For my father-in -law, James Drew and my mother-in-law, Rose Drew.
—T.L.

Text © 2008 by Madeleine Dunphy.
Illustrations © 2008 by Tom Leonard.

For information, write to:
Web of Life Children's Books
P.O. Box 2726, Berkeley, California 94702

Published in the United States in 2008 by Web of Life Children's Books.

Printed in Singapore.

Library of Congress Control Number: 2007939791

ISBN 0-9777539-4-8 (hardcover edition)
978-0-9777539-4-9

The artwork for this book was prepared using acrylic.

Read all the books in the series:
Here Is the African Savanna, *Here Is the Tropical Rain Forest*, *Here Is the Wetland*,
Here Is the Coral Reef, *Here Is the Southwestern Desert* and *Here Is the Arctic Winter*.

For more information about our books, and the authors
and artists who create them, visit our website:
www.weboflifebooks.com